70 Ways to BOOST your SELF-ESTEEM

JENNY ALEXANDER

five lanes

First published in 2017 by Five Lanes Press

Contact: info@fivelanespress.com

Text copyright © 2017 Jenny Alexander
Illustrations copyright © 2017 Karen Donnelly
Cover design copyright © 2017 Rachel Lawston

Jenny Alexander asserts her moral right to be identified as the author of this work. All rights reserved. No part of this publication may be reproduced in any form or by any means without the prior permission of the author.

This book is a simplified and updated version of The 7-Day Self-Esteem Super-Booster, published by Hodder Children's Books in 2007.

Contact: author@jennyalexander.co.uk
Website: www.jennyalexander.co.uk

ISBN:
Paperback 978-1-910300-18-3
ebook 978-1-910300-19-0

Illustration: Karen Donnelly www.karendonnelly.com
Cover design: Rachel Lawston www.lawstondesign.com

CONTENTS

About self-esteem	1
1 It's your story— be the hero!	14
2 Get goals… and get going!	24
3 Recognise your weaknesses	38
4 Build up your strengths	49
5 Take your place in the world	61
6 Say yes to life!	72
7 Celebrate being you!	84

INTRODUCTION
ABOUT SELF-ESTEEM

A lot of people think that having high self esteem means having a high opinion of yourself. They say you can boost your self-esteem by simply telling yourself all the time that you're wonderful.

If only it was as easy as that! Then all I'd have to say is

Reader – you are the most fantastic talented clever beautiful person in the whole wide world!

I could deliver the manuscript to my publisher without more ado and you could congratulate yourself on knowing all there is to know about self-esteem after reading the shortest book ever written. Hmm... tempting!

But what if you believed me? You could be in danger of developing one of the 3 Faces of False Self-esteem, and I wouldn't want that on my conscience.

THE 3 FACES OF FALSE SELF-ESTEEM

Warning: these are not a pretty sight!

First there's...

Thinking you're the bees' knees when you aren't – that's just embarrassing. It gets people hiding behind their settees when the X Factor auditions are on.

Then there's...

Thinking you're better than everyone else – that's just a pain. It makes people sit on a different table at dinnertime.

And finally there's...

Thinking you're more important than everyone else so you can push them around – that's bullying. It makes me very annoyed!

Get out of my way!

I warned you they weren't pretty!

Did you notice what the 3 Faces of False Self-esteem have in common? They're all 'thinking' things that aren't true – thinking they're the bees' knees etc. That's the thing about false self-esteem – it's based on illusions rather than reality.

REAL SELF-ESTEEM

Real self-esteem isn't about having a high opinion of yourself but about having a realistic one. For example, I actually have quite a low opinion of myself as a mathematician, but that's fair enough because I've got the maths skills of a potato. On the other hand, I know I'm a pretty good cook – you should try my sticky choccy surprise (it's a surprise if there's any left by tea-time!)

It doesn't matter what you look like or how clever you are or how popular – everyone can have real self-esteem. It can be harder for certain people than for others – for example, if you're naturally more anxious and self-critical. It can also be harder at certain times than at others – for example, if you're being picked on. But it's always doable, and having high self-esteem means you can make the best of what you've got and do the best you're capable of doing.

Meet Mal and Thomas. They're both complete brain-boxes but only one of them has high self-esteem.

Mal and Thomas

Mal wants to be an architect so he knows he's got to work hard and do well. His teacher says he's bright enough but Mal isn't really convinced.

Some of the kids in Mal's class call him 'teacher's pet', which really bothers him. He tries to stay in with them by messing around and showing off about not doing any work. Secretly, he thinks maybe it's better not to try too hard anyway, because then at least you won't feel too bad if you fail.

Thomas wants to be a vet so he needs to do well too. It doesn't really bother him that the cool boys call him swotty – he just thinks 'Yes, that's right!' Thomas knows that he might not get into vet school, but he's determined to give it his best shot.

Mal and Thomas are both boys with big dreams and bags of brains. Thomas will probably end up curing cows and healing horses, but unless Mal stops worrying so much about what other people think and finds the courage to try his best, the nearest he could get to designing buildings is living in one.

There are seven steps to high self-esteem and each one leads to treasure.

SEVEN STEPS AND SEVEN TREASURES

Step 1 Be the hero of your story
Treasure Feeling in control

Step 2 Get goals and go for them
Treasure Having ambitions and enjoying success

Step 3 Recognise your weaknesses
Treasure Not being afraid of criticism

Step 4 Build up your strengths
Treasure Real confidence from real achievements

Step 5 Take your place in the world
Treasure Respect for and from other people

Step 6 Say yes to life
Treasure Knowing you can handle whatever happens

Step 7 Celebrate being you
Treasure Loving your own uniqueness

This book has one chapter for each step on the road to high self-esteem, and each chapter finishes with 10 ways you can put the ideas into practice. That means you've got a total of 70 ways to boost your self-esteem, just like it says on the cover!

Does it sound a bit like hard work? Are you thinking you might just read the chapters and skip the tasks? Well, that would be better than nothing, but high self-esteem isn't something you can get in an instant like the answer to a maths question or a joke.

Having high self-esteem is a life skill you get better at through practice, like riding a bike. You wouldn't expect to be able to ride a bike just by reading about it. You have to actually get on the bike, wobble around, fall off a few times and crash into things, until you get the hang of it.

Once you've got it, you'll be able to steer and corner, stop and slow down without even having to think about it. If you keep practising, you might even master some fancy tricks and moves, but getting new skills means doing more practice.

TIRESOME BUT TRUE!
Practice makes perfect.

Fortunately, the 70 tasks in this book are all v. quick and simple and, unlike learning to ride a bike, they don't involve any risk to life and limb!

HOW TO DO THE TASKS

Everyone's different, so there are lots of different ways you can do the tasks:

- If you're a thorough and methodical type, you can do them all after each chapter, before you go on to the next one.

- If you're impatient, like me, and you want to whizz through the book and check out what's in it first, you can just do one or two tasks at the end of each chapter before you move on to the next one, then go back after you've finished the whole book and do the ones you've skipped.

- If you're super busy, you can spread them out and just do one each day – most of them only take ten minutes – but if you've got time on your hands, you can binge them like a box set.

- If you like doing things on your own, you can work through the 70 tasks by yourself.

- If you're a sociable type, you can do them with your best mate or a group of friends, and compare notes afterwards.

- You can go through the book with your mum or dad if you're in a family that likes doing things together, or ask your teacher to do some of the tasks with your class.

You can do most of the tasks straight away – unless, of course, you're reading secretly under the bedclothes by torchlight, when you're supposed to be asleep. But there are a few that need some planning, so you might have to make a note and come back to them.

If there are any tasks you really don't fancy doing, skip them – you aren't doing SATs in self-esteem! If there are any tasks you really enjoy, do them twice – there are absolutely no unwanted side effects ☺

Try to have a go at as many different tasks as you can. 20 tasks will make a difference – 40 will make twice the difference. The more you do, the better and more confident you'll feel.

BEFORE YOU START

1. Get a special note pad

Some of the tasks need a pen and paper (don't worry – they're all v. easy). You can scab bits of paper off your mum as you go along but if you do that you might lose them and then someone else might find them, which you might not want to happen as they will include some v. private things.

Your special note pad is like a diary – you might show it to some people but you wouldn't want the world and his dog to see it.

2. Find a secret hiding place

Not for you – for your note pad! Don't be slack and just shove it under your mattress – that's so unimaginative and besides, your mum would find it the minute she changed the sheets.

3. Make a record sheet at the back

This is for people who either like keeping record sheets or won't be able to remember which tasks they've done without one.

Just put the chapter numbers down one side and the task numbers along the top, and make some boxes for ticking them off.

Turn the page to see an example of a record sheet!

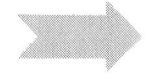

	Task 1	Task 2	Task 3	Task 4	Task 5	Task 6	Task 7	Task 8	Task 9	Task 10
Chapter 1	✓									
Chapter 2										
Chapter 3										
Chapter 4										
Chapter 5										
Chapter 6										
Chapter 7										

Besides being so flexible, the mix of talk and tasks in *70 Ways to Boost Your Self-Esteem* is brilliant because:

It's easy
All the ideas are really straightforward and the tasks are quick to do.

It's fascinating
Having a go at something new is an adventure, and when it means experimenting with the way you think about yourself and live your life, it's particularly fascinating. After all, what could be more fascinating than you?!

It works
It doesn't just puff you up with false self-esteem, filling your head with big ideas about how fantabulous you are – that might feel good for five minutes but it wouldn't last. The seven-day method works because it's rooted in real life. It's about building practical skills in a step-by-step way that you'll never forget. Just like riding a bike!

CHAPTER ONE
IT'S YOUR STORY – BE THE HERO!

Your life is like a story, with characters, scenes and events, and it's up to you what kind of role you play in it. When things go wrong, you can play the victim, feeling helpless and hard done by, or you can take control of the situation and work out what you're going to do about it, like a hero.

HERO OR VICTIM?

A hero is

- willing to have a go
- happy to set goals (good goals – it's the same basic job description for villains, except obviously they've got evil goals)
- ready to deal with difficulties
- determined to win the prize

A victim is

- reluctant to try
- unable to set goals
- afraid of setbacks
- quick to give up

Some people are heroes in their own life stories and others are victims. Which are you? Do the hero-or-victim quiz and find out.

Turn the page to do the quiz!

THE HERO-OR-VICTIM QUIZ

Your parents say you can't go on the school skiing trip because they can't afford it. What do you think?

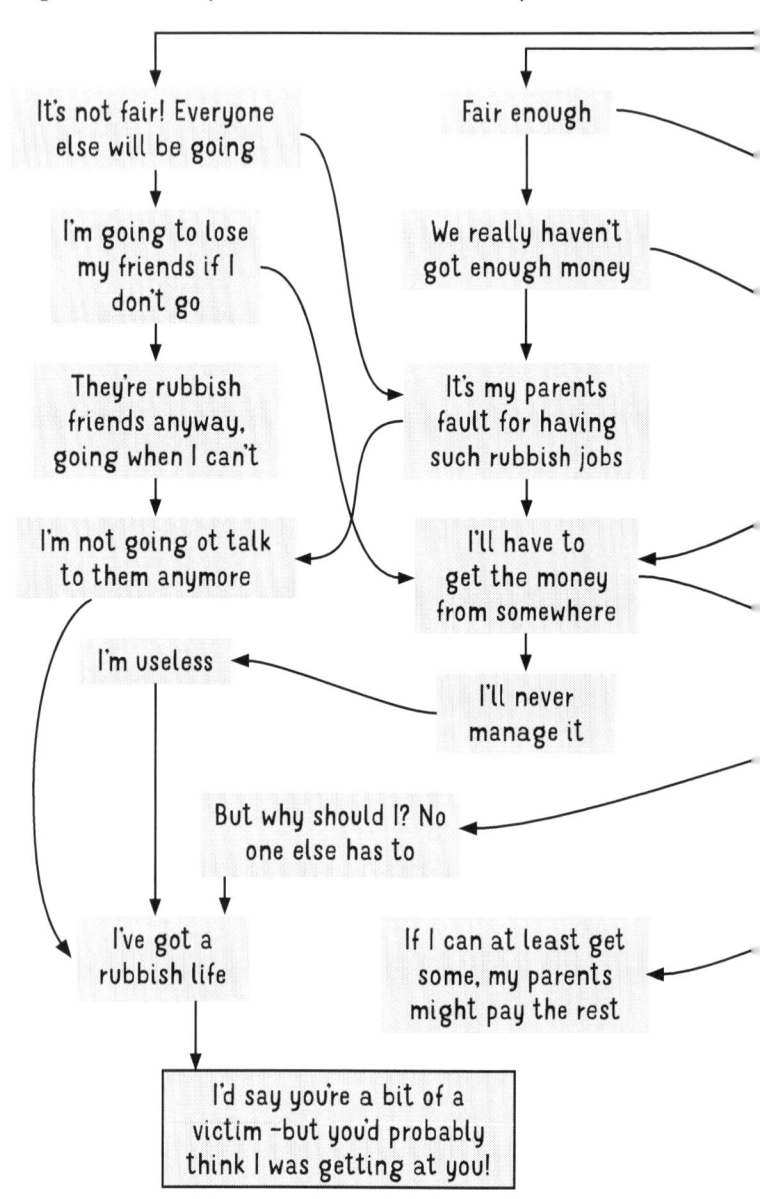

- It's not fair! Everyone else will be going
- I'm going to lose my friends if I don't go
- They're rubbish friends anyway, going when I can't
- I'm not going ot talk to them anymore

- Fair enough
- We really haven't got enough money
- It's my parents fault for having such rubbish jobs
- I'll have to get the money from somewhere
- I'll never manage it

- I'm useless
- But why should I? No one else has to
- I've got a rubbish life
- If I can at least get some, my parents might pay the rest

I'd say you're a bit of a victim – but you'd probably think I was getting at you!

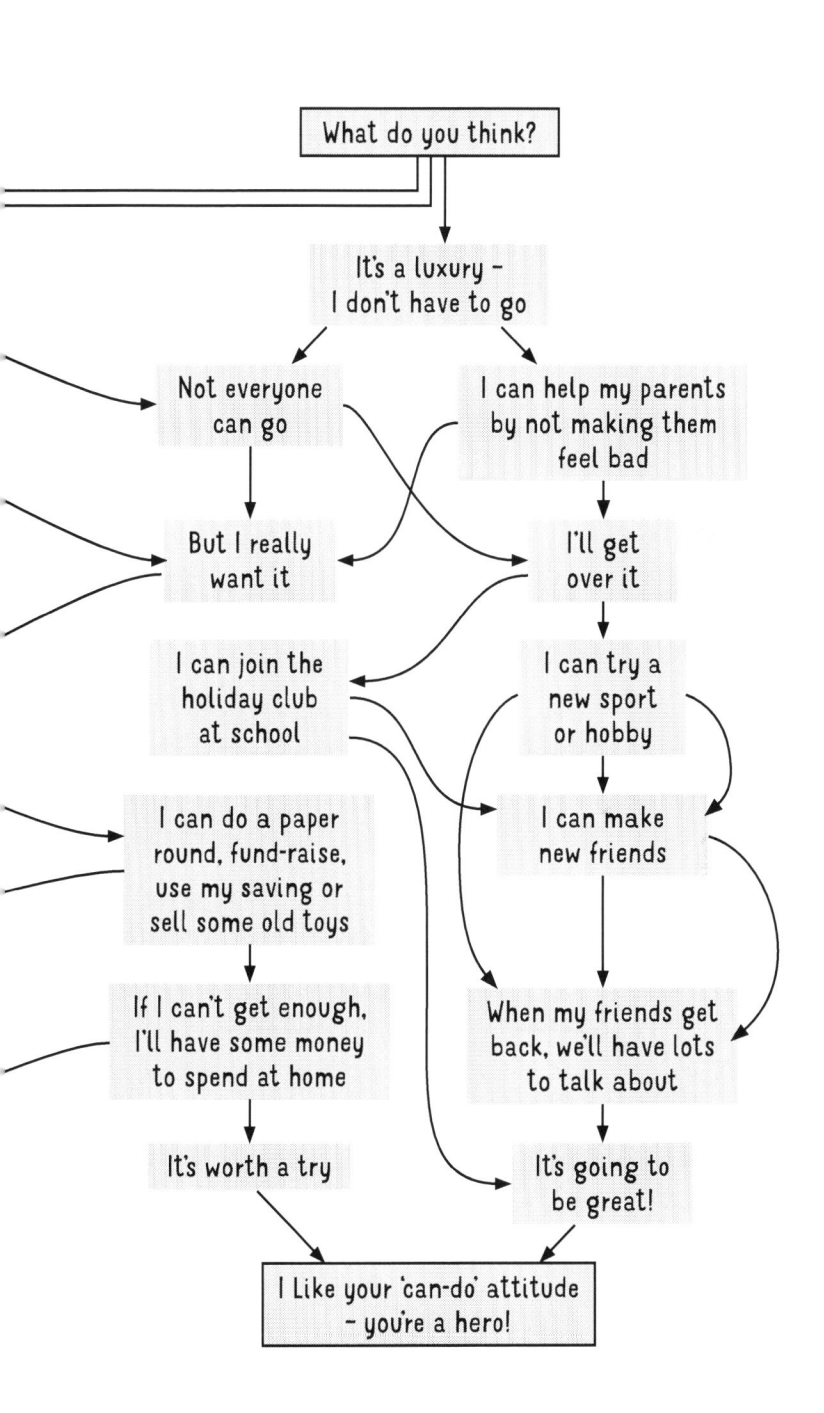

```mermaid
flowchart TD
    A[What do you think?]
    A --> B[It's a luxury – I don't have to go]
    B --> C[Not everyone can go]
    B --> D[I can help my parents by not making them feel bad]
    C --> E[But I really want it]
    D --> F[I'll get over it]
    C --> F
    D --> E
    E --> G[I can join the holiday club at school]
    F --> H[I can try a new sport or hobby]
    H --> G
    G --> I[I can do a paper round, fund-raise, use my saving or sell some old toys]
    H --> J[I can make new friends]
    G --> J
    I --> K[If I can't get enough, I'll have some money to spend at home]
    J --> L[When my friends get back, we'll have lots to talk about]
    G --> L
    H --> L
    K --> M[It's worth a try]
    L --> N[It's going to be great!]
    G --> N
    M --> O[I like your 'can-do' attitude – you're a hero!]
    N --> O
```

WHO DO YOU THINK YOU ARE?

What makes you a hero or a victim comes down to how you think about yourself.

If you're a victim you think that who you are – happy or sad, nice or nasty, successful or a failure – depends on other people and events. That makes you feel weak and vulnerable, and it also means you probably whinge a lot and blame things on everyone else, like Crystal.

Crystal

Crystal was gutted when she didn't get into drama classes at her local theatre. She complained to just about anyone who would listen and stopped talking to her mother because it was her fault that the application didn't go in on time.

Every week-end for the whole term, Crystal sat around at home feeling sorry for herself and if anyone tried to cheer her up she told them to get lost. Her Saturday afternoons were completely spoilt, she said. How was she supposed to enjoy herself when some of her friends were doing drama classes and she wasn't?

Poor Crystal!

If you're a hero you think that who you are depends entirely on yourself – you take responsibility for creating the life you want and being the person you want to be. This means you feel strong and in control, like Shayla.

Shayla

Shayla didn't get into drama classes either and she was just as disappointed as Crystal. She reckoned she needed something else to cheer her up so she went to the sports centre down the road to see what they had on offer. She decided to sign up for some trampolining sessions.

Shayla loved trampolining, plus it felt great to know that, although she could have spent her Saturdays moping around, she had actually gone out and done something about it.

The good news is, the way you look at things isn't set in stone – you can change it if you want to. Moving from being a victim to being a hero is as easy as this – watch out for 'Poor me' moments and change them to, 'What am I going to do about it? It's up to me.'

TEN WAYS TO BECOME THE HERO OF YOUR STORY

If you want to boost your self-esteem, you can't just sit around complaining – you have to make it happen. Being the hero of your story is one way of boosting your self-esteem, and here are ten ways to start.

1. Five favourite heroes

Write a list of five people you admire and look up to. This might include famous people like sports stars and actors, fictional heroes or people you know, like a relative or teacher. Don't take long over it – just write down the first five you think of.

Write one sentence each about why you admire them. They may be brave, kind, wise, honest, funny, patient, successful…

Your heroes show you things you have the potential to develop in yourself – that's why they inspire you.

2. The hero project

Who is your biggest personal hero? Write down the first person that comes into your mind – don't think about it!

Now find out some things you didn't know about them. If it's someone you know, ask questions. If it's a famous person, look online or in the library.

Seeing how your heroes achieved their success is like a road map, showing you the way.

3. The hero picture

Draw, copy or download a picture of one of your personal heroes. Put it on your bedroom wall.

4. Super you!

Draw a picture of yourself as a hero – be as over-the-top as you like. Give yourself special powers. Enjoy!

If you don't like drawing, write a description of yourself as a super-hero. Notice how it makes you feel.

5. Read a story

Stories are nearly always about people facing setbacks, conquering fears, realising their goals – in short, heroes! Read a book, and imagine yourself in the fictional hero's shoes.

If you don't like reading stories, watch an adventure film instead.

6. Your hero story

Write the story of something you did that you feel proud of – for example, helping a friend, doing a great piece of schoolwork, trying something new. Show why it was a challenge, what was hard about it, and how you overcame any obstacles.

Do this as a picture strip if you don't really like writing.

7. Check the label!

Without even noticing it, we all label ourselves and then we believe what it says on the label. Finish the following sentence in three different ways to reflect the negative thoughts you have about yourself – 'I am….' For example, 'I am selfish ', 'I am lazy', 'I am stupid'

Write down the positive opposite. 'I am selfless, I am resourceful, I am clever' – feels better, doesn't it?

Say it to yourself in the mirror 10 times, nice and slowly, giving yourself time to really notice all the ways the new labels are just as true as the old ones.

People with low self-esteem often say 'I wish I was someone else' – well you can be! Just switch labels.

8. Three totem animals

Every hero has special powers and here's how you can find out what yours are.

Write down your three favourite animals – the first ones that come to mind. Write them down and then add the positive characteristics you associate with each one. For example

> **Lion**: strong, fearless
> **Dolphin**: friendly, sociable
> **Grasshopper**: lively, hard to spot

These are your special powers, and thinking about your totem animals can help you to develop them.

9. Your animal guide

Draw, copy or download a picture of your favourite animal, or make a little model of it from fimo or clay. While you are doing it, think about why you like it so much.

Keep your picture or model by your bedside or carry it around in your pocket and let your animal inspire you to develop its best quality in yourself.

10. It's up to you

Draw a nice big dot on one of your fingernails. Every time you notice it throughout the day remind yourself that no-one else is responsible for the way you are – it's up to you.

CHAPTER TWO
GET GOALS... AND GET GOING!

You need goals to give you a sense of purpose and direction in life, even though you might not always achieve them. It's a bit like in football – you're always going for the goal and it's great when one goes in, but you can enjoy the game even if you don't score at all.

Trying to live without goals would be like trying to play football without goals. How pointless and confusing would that feel? Yet people with low self-esteem do exactly that. They don't dare to set themselves goals and really try, because they're too scared they might fail.

Patrick

Patrick loved rock music and all his greatest heroes were drummers. He knew their names and studied their techniques, trying out different rhythms on the table and tapping with his feet.

Patrick couldn't think of anything but drumming, yet if anyone asked him what he wanted to do when he left school, he would shrug his shoulders and say he didn't know.

Even when his parents asked him if he'd like to be a drummer, he shook his head. What was the point in dreaming? He'd never be good enough.

Patrick's dad offered to find him a drumming class, but Patrick didn't want him to, because he thought the other kids might be much better than him. Maybe they'd laugh at him for trying and how bad would that feel?

But because all he could think about was drumming, nothing else really interested him at all, and while his mates were off doing all kinds of other things – Jub with his funny blog, Amy with her gymnastics club, Sam with the Sea Scouts – Patrick just sat around tapping on tables, not even daring to dream.

People with high self-esteem are scared of failing too, but that doesn't stop them trying – it makes them even more determined to succeed. Like being a victim or a hero, how good you are at going for goals is all a question of attitude.

What's your attitude towards failure? Could fear of failure be holding you back? Do this Little Tick Test and find out.

THE LITTLE TICK TEST

Tick the statements that apply to you.

When I try hard and fail I think…

1. I wish I hadn't bothered. ☐

2. This proves I'll never do it. ☐

3. I feel embarrassed I tried something I couldn't do. ☐

4. People will think I'm stupid. ☐

5. I'm not going to do that again. ☐

6. I'm glad I had a go. ☐

7. This shows I need to find another way. ☐

8. I feel proud of myself for trying even though it was hard. ☐

9. Other people can think what they like. ☐

10. I'm not going to give up. ☐

RESULTS:

Numbers 1-5 are low self esteem attitudes towards failure and if you got any ticks at all here it's time for a rethink.

Numbers 6-10 are the attitudes you need and, if you've got them, there will be no stopping you!

....

Everyone's scared of failing and the best way to overcome that fear is by thinking of failure as simply a step on the way to success. Be like Thomas Edison who invented the light bulb – he tried gazillions of experiments before he reached his goal but he didn't regard any of them as failures – he said they were all successful attempts at finding out what didn't work!

SETTING GOALS

There are two kinds of goals – long-term goals and short-term goals.

Long-term goals aren't going to happen straight away, but you can set short-term goals right now that will help you move towards them. For example:

....
DATE – JULY 9TH

LONG TERM GOAL
To get in the school netball team when the league starts in October.

SHORT TERM GOALS
Today

Go for a run to get fitter. Choose healthy option at dinnertime.

This week
- Get Dad to fix my netball hoop to the garage wall.
- Do shooting practice.
- See if any of my mates want to try for the team too.
- Run on at least four days, choose healthy dinners but let myself have chips on Friday. (I'm only human!)

This month
- When school holidays start, run every day.

- Practise hoops half an hour a day, except when it's raining.
- Read up on the rules.
- Get some mates over for a throw-around.

∙∙∙

There are three rules for goal setting:

1. Be precise

Not just 'to be good at netball' but 'to get in the school netball team'.

2 Set a time-scale

'When the league starts in October.'
'Today, this week, this month…'

3 Keep a record

This helps you to stay on course because, if you get despondent, it reminds you how far you've come.

Your record might look something like this.

∙∙∙

RECORD OF PROGRESS

July 9th – went for a run, had salad for dinner.

July 10th – went for a run, had jacket potato and beans, asked Dad to fix netball hoop to garage wall.

July 11th – went for a run, had tuna and tomato sandwich, reminded Dad about hoop.

July 12th – Dad fixed hoop, and we had a throw-around (he's rubbish!).

Asked the gang if anyone else wants to try for the team – Lisa, Kerri and Jiya said yes.

July 13th – L, K, J and me all went for a run after school.

July 14th – got a book out the library to mug up on the rules…

. . . .

I hope you noticed a very important thing about this record, and that is that even if you don't make the team in October, it's still a record of achievement.

DON'T BE AFRAID TO MOVE THE GOAL POSTS!

From time to time, review your long-term goals, and see if you need to change them. This can happen if:

- You've achieved what you set out to do.

For example, when you've got your half mile swimming certificate maybe you could go for the mile.

- You've discovered something you'd rather do instead.

For example, supposing you wanted to be in a band but found you preferred handing out fliers to standing up on stage, then your new goal might be to help organise gigs, rather than play in them.

- You've realised you aren't going to manage it.

Let's face it, this can happen – so if you've given it your best shot, be glad you had a go and put it down to experience.

THREE IFS (INTERESTING FACTS)

1. If at first you don't succeed, try, try, and try again.
2. If at first you do succeed – you need harder goals!
3. If you never succeed at all, you need more realistic goals!

COURAGE, ACTION... SUCCESS!

People who manage to overcome their fear of failure and really go for what they want are bound to be more successful, and success is a top tonic for your self-esteem.

TWO MORE IFS

1. If you try, you might not achieve your goal.

2. If you don't try you certainly won't achieve it.

TEN WAYS TO GET GOALS AND GO FOR THEM

Getting goals and having the courage to go for them is one way to boost your self-esteem Here are ten little mini goals, so you can start right now!

1. The might-not-like-it list

Write down 5 things you haven't tried because you think you might not like them... and then try one.

For example:

- Those veggie pies they sometimes have at school dinner
- A new sitcom on TV
- Not-your-usual weekly magazine
- Going fishing with your dad
- Wearing something yellow

Note: These should be things you definitely could do if you tried.

2. The mission statement

Think of a long-term goal and write a mission statement by filling in these gaps – 'I want to …. because…'

Be specific and give as many reasons as you like.

For example, 'I want to climb Ben Nevis because my dad's done it and it's the highest mountain in the UK and also…'

Note: This doesn't have to be 'realistic' – dare to dream!

3. The might-not-be-very-good-at-it list

Write down five things you'd like to do but haven't tried, because you think you might not be very good at them.

For example:

- That new computer game your mate's always going on about
- Joining in with class discussions
- Cooking your own scrambled eggs
- Swimming club
- Writing an article for the school magazine

When you try something new, you probably won't be very good at first – but if you don't try, how will you learn?

4. Go for goal!

Football, netball, hockey…take part in any game that has goals. Feel the excitement, energy and sense of purpose that going for a goal gives you, even if you don't score.

If you can't take part in a game, get the buzz just by watching your favourite team play.

5. Your perfect day

This is nice!

Sit quietly and take a few minutes to imagine your perfect day. Where would you be? Who would be with you? What would you be doing?

Start with waking up in the morning and go right through to bedtime, giving yourself everything you could possibly desire.

Write it down, using the present tense, or make a picture strip. 'It's a lovely sunny morning and the smell of bacon is wafting up from the kitchen. After breakfast, the limo comes to take me and Freddie to the airport…'

Your perfect day shows you what's really important to you, and could give you ideas about future goals.

6. The game plan

Think of a long-term goal and work out a plan of action. Set some short-term goals that can help you work towards it. Include one that you could do right away – and do it!

For example:

LONG-TERM GOAL

- I want to cut my TV viewing down to 2 hours a night by the end of the month.

SHORT-TERM GOALS

Today

- Look through the TV Guide and put circles round the programmes I really want to watch this week

This week

- Only watch the programmes I circled
- See if anyone else in the family wants to join in...

You get the idea.

7. Have a new day

Mostly, we keep things safe by doing the same old things every day – how boring!

Have a new day by:

1. Chatting to someone you don't usually talk to.
2. Eating something you've never tried before.

3. Wearing something you've never worn before – you can borrow this from a mate or someone in your family.

8. Now, forever, never

Get together with some mates or family members. Give everyone three identical pieces of paper. All write down something you'd like to do right now on one piece, something you'd like to do all your life on the second piece and something you wouldn't like to do at all on the third. For example" 'Now – look cool'; 'Forever – Live in a huge house'; 'Never – Go bog-snorkelling'

Mix the pieces of paper up, then take turns to choose one and try to guess who wrote it. If you guess right, you get to keep the piece of paper but if you're wrong you have to put it back in the middle. The one with the most pieces of paper at the end wins.

Note: If you pick your own, put it back and choose another one.

9. Have a go

Try a new sport, game, hobby or activity.

If you don't try new things you might be missing out on something you've got natural talent for, and even if it turns out you're a complete chump at chess, you'll feel good knowing you had the courage to give it a go.

10. Experience success

Choose one of your long-term goals. Imagine that you have just achieved it. Everyone's congratulating you, everyone's celebrating. Have you just made your first speech in the House of Commons? The MPs are all cheering and saying 'Here, here!' Have you won a big prize for your poetry? The cameras are flashing, the audience is on its feet!

Close your eyes and really be there. Notice all your senses – what can you see, hear, touch, smell, taste? Take your time.

Feels great, doesn't it? Imagining success is a great incentive to achieving it.

CHAPTER THREE
RECOGNISE YOUR WEAKNESSES

Nobody's perfect. Even heroes have faults and weaknesses along with their super-powers because they're human beings, not gods. Recognising your weaknesses is a kind of strength. Look what happened to the legendary Greek hero Achilles when he got too full of himself and thought he couldn't be beaten.

Achilles and his famous heel

When he was born, Achilles' mum took him to the sacred River Styx and dipped him in, because the water had magic properties that could make a person immortal. Unfortunately, the heel she held him by when she dipped him didn't get wet, and therefore that part of his body remained vulnerable.

Achilles grew up to have loads of adventures and kill loads of enemies, and it seemed like nothing could hurt him, so he got puffed up with pride. But then another hero came along called Paris… and Paris had done his homework. He shot a poisoned arrow into Achilles' heel and Paf! Achilles died.

To feel safe and strong in the world you need to:

- Recognise your weaknesses ('Oh, oh – dodgy heel!')
- Do something about them ('I know – I'll fix a rear view mirror to my helmet…')

RECOGNISING YOUR WEAKNESSES

There are lots of human weaknesses to choose from – meanness, selfishness, jealousy, arrogance, cruelty, thoughtlessness… to name but a few. Everyone is capable of acting meanly, selfishly etc, but most of the time we don't like to admit it.

We make excuses – 'OK, so I did say you looked like the leftovers table at a jumble sale but that was just a slip of the tongue' – or we blame somebody else – 'I did say you were stupid but it's your own fault because you are!'

The great thing about recognising your weaknesses is that it means you don't have to worry so much about people criticising you.

Jaimie

Jaimie fell out with her best friend, Beth, and, out of revenge, she told another girl something that Beth had made her promise to keep secret.

At first, Jaimie thought it served Beth right, but then she began to feel bad about it.

When Beth told Jaimie, 'I'm glad I'm not friends with you any more. You're a rubbish friend!' Jaimie could have felt upset and hurt. After all they had been through together! How could Beth say something like that about her?

But instead of bristling under Beth's criticism, Jaimie just owned up. 'I know. It was a horrible thing to do, even if we aren't friends any more, and I'm sorry.'

Another reason it's a shame not to recognise your weaknesses is that you can learn from them. Say you recognise that you were being sulky refusing to take part in the panto just because you didn't get the lead role, then you can think, 'Maybe sulkiness is a problem for me. What can I do about it?'

DOING WHAT YOU CAN DO

Owning up to your faults and failings can be hard because it means you may have to swallow your pride, apologise and try to make amends.

It takes courage too, because it makes you feel uncomfortable. But don't worry, that's how it should be – feeling bad is what makes you decide not to behave like that again. It goes like this:

- I was unkind.
- I feel bad about saying those nasty things.
- I don't want to feel like this again!
- Hmm…
- Maybe I'd better not say nasty things.

In this way you can let your faults and failings teach you to do things better.

A WORD OF WARNING

Don't let your lovely helpful Inner Teacher – the little voice inside that says 'Tut tut – that wasn't very nice!' – turn into a hideous Harsh Judge

Sure, you should feel bad when you've done something wrong because that's what makes you decide not to do it again, but don't keep beating yourself up about it – and definitely don't think that it proves you're a bad person. You're only human!

Wallowing in shame doesn't get you anywhere – it actually stops you from doing anything about your faults and failings because then everything gets stuck like this:

- I was unkind.
- I feel bad about saying those nasty things.
- I feel really, really bad.
- I must be a nasty person…

If you start on this downwards spiral of shame, thinking your faults and failings make you a bad person, you end up putting all your energy into gathering evidence to support the case against yourself instead of learning from your mistake and doing something about it.

- I'm a nasty person because I said mean things…
- And come to think of it, I also did a mean thing letting my bro take the blame when I trod on the phone…

- And then there was the time I told everyone my best mate's secret... And besides that...

Ahem! Excuse me... is all this self-criticism actually producing a result for you or the mates you were mean to? More to the point, since this book is called '70 Ways to Boost Your Self-esteem' – is it helping your self-esteem? No! So just don't go there. Take action!

THE FAULTS AND FAILINGS ACTION PLAN

Self-esteem isn't about being perfect but about being the best that you can be and, as weaknesses like selfishness and pride are part of human nature, it's a lifelong challenge.

You can rise to the challenge in a simple 5-step way:

1. Accept you're not perfect and you can be wrong.

2. When you do something wrong – admit it.

3. Don't get stuck in self-criticism.

4. Say sorry and make amends.

5. Try not to do it again.

It's straightforward – but that doesn't mean it's easy. It takes courage and commitment, and that means that if you can manage it you will feel rightly good about yourself. That's why recognising your weaknesses is a really important step on the path to high self-esteem.

TEN WAYS TO RECOGNISE YOUR WEAKNESSES

Recognising your weaknesses is one way to boost your self-esteem, and here are ten ways you can start doing that right now. Some of them are tough, but I have every faith in you. You can do them!

1. I don't like... oh!
Think of someone you don't like – it can be someone you know or someone famous. Write down three things you don't like about them. For example – I don't like Amy because she's a drama queen plus she never thinks of anybody else, plus she can't keep a secret.

That's the easy bit! Now comes the hard bit. Think of times when you have done each of the three things in your list. 'Oh – I suppose I did make a bit of a fuss when I thought that wasp had gone up my sweatshirt...'

2. Don't judge other people
This is about the Horrible Harsh Judge, that critical voice inside you telling you you're bad or stupid just because you made a mistake. He builds

up muscle by criticising other people, so you can cut him down to size by absolutely refusing to criticise anyone else.

Some people won't find this at all hard and will be able to keep it up all day – some people will struggle to last five minutes. So I'll leave it up to you to set your own time-scale for this task – you know yourself better than I do!

3. I wish I hadn't done that…

Write down something you did that you wish you hadn't done. For example, *I took a ten pound note that was lying around in my sister's bedroom.*

- What were the consequences? *She spent two hours turning her room upside down looking for it. I felt really guilty…*

- What could you have done about it? *I could have owned up, said sorry and given it back – but I like living too much.*

- What did you do about it? *Er… nothing.*

- What did you learn? *I've never picked up money that didn't belong to me again.*

You'll notice with this little task that even if you didn't quite have the courage to own up, you can still learn from your mistakes.

4. Mistakes and lessons

Think of 3 times you did something you felt bad about. What did you learn from them?

5. Check out your private put-downs

Be a detective and put a trail on yourself all day. Keep your ear to the ground for any private put-downs you make. Take a note. For example, you might forget your packed lunch and think, 'I'm so stupid!'

Notice whether you criticise yourself or your mistakes – it was stupid to forget your lunch, but that doesn't make you a stupid person. You are bigger than your mistakes.

6. The antidote

What's your worst weakness? If you can't think of anything, what do people most often criticise you for? For example – 'I can be bossy'

Choose one of the following:

- To try and go all day without giving in to your weakness – for example, without being bossy.

- To do one thing during the day which is the opposite of your weakness – for example, letting someone else be in charge.

7. Flip the coin

Strengths and weaknesses are two sides of the same coin, and often the things we dislike about ourselves can conceal a secret strength.

Write down three things you think of as weaknesses (they don't have to be your own) Find some ways in which they could be considered a strength. For example –

Rudeness – can come from wanting to hurt people, but can also come from speaking your mind.

Possible strength – honesty (Simon Cowell on *X Factor* might be an example of this).

8. Thumbs up

Repeat this sentence to yourself every time you think of it during the day:

> I'm not perfect but I'm fine

You can remember it by using your fingers. Open your hand and fold your fingers in one by one, starting with your thumb, as you say the words, 'I'm not… perfect… but… I'm…'

Then stick your thumb up again and say 'fine!'

This is a sort of benign brainwashing and it works. It's also great exercise for the muscles in your hands!

9. Not just the gorgeous bits

The famous French author Stendhal said that when you truly love someone you love them 'warts and all'. He meant that you love the whole person, not just the gorgeous bits.

Think of somebody you love – say, your mate Molly.

What are their weaknesses? *Well, she's a bit scatterbrained…*

What would they be like without those weaknesses? *She wouldn't be Molly (but she might be able to find two matching socks in the morning!).*

Notice how you love them 'warts and all.'

Wart note: A wart is a hard little spot on the skin. Don't worry if you get one – they're very common and completely harmless.

10. Love your warts!

- Write down three of your own weaknesses.
- What would you be like without them?
- Can you love yourself, 'warts and all'?

CHAPTER FOUR
BUILD UP YOUR STRENGTHS

Self-confidence is an important element of high self-esteem. You can't get it by just puffing yourself up – that's empty self-confidence and it can:

- Put you in danger – like if you think you know all about hang-gliding so you don't bother listening to the instructor.
- Make people laugh at you – like the Emperor's new clothes.

THE EMPEROR'S NEW CLOTHES

There was once an Emperor who loved having nice things to wear. One day, two tailors offered to make him a fabulous new suit out of magic cloth, a cloth so fine that stupid people wouldn't be able to see it at all.

The Emperor knew he wasn't stupid and he couldn't wait to see the beautiful magic cloth so he told them to go ahead. The two tailors pretended to weave and sew, and then took the pretend suit of clothes to the Emperor.

The Emperor thought, I can't see anything at all, but I don't want them to think I'm stupid so I'd better pretend I can. He stripped off and let them dress him in the non-existent clothes.

Everyone in the court thought, I can't see anything at all, but I don't want to look stupid so I'd better pretend I can. And they all clapped and complimented the Emperor on his wonderful good taste.

But a little child in the crowd piped up – 'The Emperor's got nothing on!' Which kind of put everybody on the spot. Embarrassing, or what?

....

True self-confidence doesn't come from pretending – it comes from a realistic understanding of your own abilities. But just like recognising your weaknesses, recognising your strengths can sometimes be difficult especially if you're a bit low on self-confidence.

Strengths come in two varieties:

- Skills and knowledge
- Personal qualities

You're bound to have plenty of both.

SKILLS AND KNOWLEDGE

Skills and knowledge come out of your everyday experience but you might not even notice them because:

- *Once you've mastered something, you do it without even thinking about it*

For example, supposing you've got a dog, you'll know loads of stuff about keeping dogs that people like me don't know, such as how often they need feeding, how much exercise they need and how to stop them leaving little heaps on the carpet.

- *Most people think competitively*

'OK,' you may say, 'so I can play hockey, but I can't play well enough to make the team so I must be rubbish.' No, no! You can still play hockey – you know the rules, you can wield the stick, you can hit the ball – this is real knowledge and real skills.

If you've got this far with *70 Ways to Boost Your Self-esteem*, you can certainly read and write – and those are fabulous skills that absolutely everybody under-estimates unless they always come top in class.

- *The things you're best at aren't always the ones that are most highly valued within your family or at school*

Supposing you love drawing but your family think art's a waste of time? Supposing you're more into making friends than doing schoolwork – too bad you never get graded on being a great friend.

In this case, you might recognise that you have ability but you might not recognise how much it's worth.

PERSONAL QUALITIES

Good personal qualities like patience and kindness are part of human nature and that means everyone's got them. But we often don't recognise them in ourselves because:

- *We think everyone just should be good*

In an ideal world where everything was how it should be, being good would be nothing special.

But in the real world, it's a choice. You can be mean if you want to, you can be lazy, aggressive, impatient, rude – so if you decide to try to play to your best qualities instead, that's a positive choice you can feel good about.

- *We think it has to be 24:7*

This means we don't give ourselves credit for the times we show kindness, patience or whatever – we just beat ourselves up about the times that we don't.

Obviously, it would be nice if we could all be lovely 24:7, but in the real world? Not possible! So when you get it right, give yourself a pat on the back.

- *We don't want to get too full of ourselves*

Modesty is an admirable quality, but I want to put in a good word at this point for pride. Pride gets a bad press sometimes, with people saying things like 'Pride comes before a fall', but it's actually a good and proper response to personal achievement.

Being proud of yourself when you get things right doesn't mean you're in danger of getting too full of yourself, for the simple reason that you won't get things right all the time.

So when you do, head up, chest out, shoulders back – enjoy your moment.

Self-esteem means feeling OK about yourself and that's an awful lot easier if you really notice all the great skills and qualities you've got going for you.

TEN WAYS TO BUILD UP YOUR STRENGTHS

Recognising your skills, knowledge and positive personal qualities is one way to boost your self-esteem, and here are ten ways to start building up those strengths.

1. Your special skills list

Write a list of ten things you've got special skills in. If you find them hard to spot, think about:

- Your hobbies and interests.

- What you do at weekends and on holiday – for example camping, going abroad, shopping.
- Your home situation – for example, living in a big or small family, keeping pets, the things other family members are interested in.

Lots of these will be things you take for granted because they're normal for you – but they aren't part of everybody's life.

2. Your dream hobby

People are best at things they love doing – and that's why having a hobby is so great for your self-confidence.

Think of a hobby you'd like to try but haven't got around to yet. If it's something you might be able to start straight away, like swimming or singing in a choir, ask your mum or dad to help you find out what opportunities are available in your local area.

Libraries, schools, sports centres and theatres often have information about community projects, or you could look on your local government website.

If it's something you can't start straight away, like scuba diving, find out as much as you can about it from books and websites.

3. 'Who am I?'

Write a kenning called 'Who am I? A kenning is a poem in which every line has two words and every second word ends –er. For example

Who am I?

Book writer
Rabbit keeper
Wild walker
Curry lover
Friend supporter
Joke teller...

Keep it positive, make it as long as you like, and finish it off with a rhyme

Great speller!

Note: You can switch the lines around if that makes it easier to end with a rhyme.

Another note: Now you can add 'writing kennings' to your skills list – and 'kenning writer' to your kenning!

4. Nice things people say

Lots of people find it very hard to take a compliment. They get embarrassed or think the person is just trying to be nice.

Write down three complimentary things your

friends, teachers or family members have said about you. Put your self-doubt on one side and accept them at face value. Smile!

5. Mirror, mirror

Write down five things you like about yourself and say them in front of a mirror when no one is around. 'I laugh a lot, I like my hair, I'm not scared of trying new things…'

6. One skill under the microscope

Think of something that you know a lot about because it's been part of your everyday life, such as living in the country or playing fantasy football.

Put this special skill under the microscope and jot down all the things you know about it.

For example, I used to have a rabbit that lived indoors. I know how to house-train a rabbit, feed it, groom it and make toys for it. I know why rabbits 'chin' the furniture and sometimes try to put their head under your foot…

There's a lot more besides but I expect you want to get on and put one of your own skills under the microscope, so I won't keep you!

7. The most famous speech in the world about having the courage to shine

Read this extract from the speech that Nelson Mandela, the black South African leader gave when he was released from prison. Copy it out, so that you can remember it.

It is our light, not our darkness, that most frightens us.

We ask ourselves:

'Who am I to be brilliant, gorgeous, talented, fabulous?'

Actually, who are you not to be?

You are a child of God.

Your playing small doesn't serve the world.

---

8. Share your wisdom

You can get knowledge from reading a book, but you get wisdom by learning from experience. That's why old people are supposed to be wise, because they've had lots of experiences to learn from.

But you don't have to be old to have wisdom. For example, you know from experience what it's like going to school, which someone who has never been yet doesn't know.

Write a page of advice for someone who's four or five years old, and about to start school for the very first time. Tell them about register and lessons and reading corner and playtime... all the things you remember about being in Reception class.

Enjoy the fact that you can help and reassure someone younger than you because you've got the wisdom of experience.

This is pretty much exactly what I did with my book, *Going Up! The No-Worries Guide to Secondary School,* but for older children, obviously. If you're already at secondary school, write a page of advice for someone who is just about to move up.

9. Personal pride

Think of something you've done that you feel proud of. It doesn't have to be anything earth shattering. Success is a personal thing, and how proud you should feel is related to how hard it was for you to achieve. For example, I was bitten by a German Shepherd dog when I was little and one of my proudest achievements is overcoming my fear of dogs.

10. A message to your mind

This task is so simple and quick you might think it can't possibly work – but it does!

First...

Think of a personal quality you wish you had more of, for example, 'I wish I was more patient.'

Write it down in the present tense as if

you've already got it – 'Right now, I am a really patient person!'

Repeat it to yourself ten times at least three times during the day, including just before you go to bed.

It doesn't matter if it sounds nuts to you – simply saying the words plants a seed in your unconscious mind that will blossom and grow.

CHAPTER FIVE
TAKE YOUR PLACE IN THE WORLD

'No man is an island, entire of itself: every man is a piece of the continent, a part of the main…'

That's a quote from John Donne, a v. famous poet from the seventeenth century (I like to get a bit of culture in my books!). Although it's nearly 400 years since he wrote it, people still repeat it because it contains a really important truth – that we can't exist on our own.

Because everyone depends on each other, self-esteem isn't just about having a good opinion of yourself as an individual, but also as a member of society.

MY HOUSE, MY STREET, MY COUNTRY, THE WORLD!

Did you ever do that thing that lots of kids do when they first learn how to write their address?

> Miss Ellie Jane Maria Josie Martin
> Flat 5
> Ambrosia House
> Beehive Street
> Wimbledon
> London
> SW19 4BQ
> England
> Great Britain
> Europe
> The World

You know – adding all the extra bits?

Well it actually makes quite a nice list of communities that you are part of. First, there's your family, then your neighbourhood, then your suburb, then your city – or if you live in the country, your village and nearest town. You are also part of your country, your continent and the whole human race.

There are other communities that you belong to as well, like your school, class, church, football club and so on.

THE THREE Rs

In education the three Rs are Reading, Riting and Rithmetic (I don't know who invented this but I think they need to go back to school!). When it comes to living in communities, the three Rs are Rules, Rights and Responsibilities.

Rules are what hold everything together. It might feel as if rules restrict your personal power and freedom, but actually they protect it. Rules mean that you have rights.

Here are some examples of your rights:

- In this country, kids have the right to go to school and not be exploited in the labour market.

- Everyone has the right not to be attacked by other people or have their property stolen.

- In schools, a rule like 'no running in the corridors' means you have the right to walk around without getting trampled on.

But if you want to have rights you've got to accept some responsibilities.

Responsibilities arise because everyone is equal under the law. We've all got the same rights, so the no-running-in-the-corridors rule doesn't only give you the right not to be trampled on – it also gives everyone else the right not to be trampled on by you. It's your right not to be trampled on but it's your responsibility not to trample on other people.

R YOU UP FOR THE THREE Rs?

You might say, 'I don't care about that rule – I'm the biggest kid in school!' But if you start to pick and choose and just obey the rules you like, that opens the door for everyone else to do the same, and they will all have different views about which rules they don't want to bother with.

Society works when everyone pulls together. If you undermine the rules that make your community strong, you're actually undermining your own rights within it.

You can't choose the rules, but you can choose what values you want to live by. For example, it isn't illegal to be mouthy and rude – you can do it if you want. It isn't illegal to tell lies, tease people and play mean tricks.

YOUR VALUES

What do you personally believe in? What are your priorities? You might care passionately about the natural world, and believe that we should all recycle as much of our waste as we can. You might think it's wrong to eat meat, and we should all be vegetarians. You might think it's important to be kind and helpful to each other.

Your beliefs are part of who you are, and being willing to stand up for them is brilliant for your self-esteem.

Daniel

Daniel and his mates found Sophie's mobile phone on the school playing field. The others wanted to read her messages for a laugh before they gave it back.

Daniel wasn't comfortable about it. A person's messages were private like a diary and just because they had found her phone, that didn't give them the right to pry.

The others called Daniel a goody-goody and started opening Sophie's messages anyway. They laughed and said 'Oooh…' at the first one as if it was really interesting, just to make Daniel feel left out. Daniel did feel left out, but as he went off to find something else to do, he also felt proud of himself for doing the right thing.

Doing the right thing means following your heart and deciding what you believe in. If you think we should recycle more – do it. Wash out your family's jam jars and buy your clothes from charity shops. If you think we should eat less meat, become a vegetarian. If you want a gentler, more caring society, be polite to your neighbours and do some voluntary work. Have the courage of your convictions.

We create and nurture the societies we live in, and our societies create and nurture us. Being part of something good feels good. Group hug!

TEN WAYS TO TAKE YOUR PLACE IN THE WORLD

Understanding that you aren't alone, and you have an important role to play, is one way to boost your self-esteem – so here are ten ways to take your place in the world.

1. Who are you?

Write your address, putting in all the extra bits. Then make a list of all the organisations you belong to.

See how they help to define who you are by going through each one, starting with 'I am…'

For example, 'I am from Govan... I am a Glaswegian... I am a Scot... I am British... I am a European... I am part of the human race. I am a St Mary's pupil... I am a member of Saturday Club.'

2. Power people

Adults have more power in the world than kids and that can be a good thing for you. Write down five adults you could talk to if you needed help with a problem.

What are their special powers? For example, life experience, knowledge of the local area, role in society (teacher, policeman, doctor etc.).

How could their powers help you?

3. Your ideal world – picture it!

Get a nice big piece of paper – stick several pieces together if you've only got titchy ones to hand.

Draw yourself in the middle – looking good of course, great big smile.

Surround yourself with scenes of people behaving how you'd like them to in your ideal world. If you like, label them (this could be a good idea if you're artistically challenged and your 'Person clearing up her dog's mess' looks more like she's about to thwack the poor pooch with her shovel).

4. Do as you would be done by

This is your chance to write the rules! List five people and put what they must not do. For example:

- My brother must not borrow my stuff without asking.
- My mum must not shout at me.
- Kids at school must not call me names.

Now turn them round like this:

- I must not borrow my bro's stuff without asking.
- I must not shout at my mum.
- I must not call kids at school names.

5. Make a gift

You can do this even if you haven't got much money. For example, if you get a few pence change at the shops, put it in the charity box on the counter. Take your old books and magazines along to your local health centre or dentist's surgery to put in their waiting room. Give toys or clothes you don't want to a charity shop or jumble sale.

6. Quality time

Give your parents some quality time. I know you're busy, but most parents really appreciate it. Make your mum a cup of tea and ask her about her day.

Or see if your dad would like to play a video game with you.

7. Your social map

Draw a smiley in the middle of a piece of paper – this is you!

Surround yourself with the names of all your family members – parents, brothers, sisters, grandparents, aunts, uncles, cousins, step-dad, step-mum, step-brothers, step-sisters... everyone you can think of.

Now, all around them, using a different colour, write the names of everyone you know at school – friends, teachers, helpers... even enemies if you've got some.

Using another different colour again, write everyone else you can think of around the outside of your school people – neighbours, members of clubs you belong to, friends of your family, your doctor, dentist, social worker, church official...

You're joined to all these people simply by knowing them, even if sometimes you feel like you're all alone.

8. Give positive feedback

Nothing could be easier than this! If you enjoyed a particular lesson or assembly, tell your teacher. If you loved your family pizza night, tell your mum and dad. If you think your mates are just the best – tell them. 'Thank you' is the best gift in the world.

You're already thinking it – just say it out loud.

9. Play stuck-in-the-mud

This is a great game for showing how pulling together makes everyone stronger.

First decide who's going to be 'it' – then run like the wind!

If you get tagged, stand still with your arms out, as if you're stuck in the mud.

Any fellow player who isn't stuck can free you by touching your arm – but it's risky because the person who's 'it' will be guarding you.

If you all get stuck in the mud, the person who's 'it' wins.

Stuck-in-the-mud version two is good fun too – instead of holding your arms out when you get tagged, you have to stand with your feet apart, and people can only free you by crawling through your legs.

10. Make a paper chain

Take a long thin strip of paper and fold it concertina fashion.

Draw a person with their arms going right up to the folded edges. Cut round it, keeping the paper folded.

It looks like one person, but when you open it out – hey presto! 'No man is an island...'

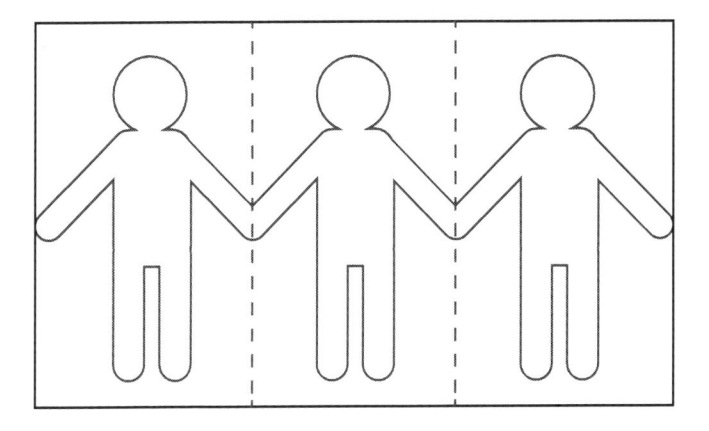

CHAPTER SIX
SAY YES TO LIFE!

A hero is big... a society is bigger... but now we come to something really, really, really huge...

LIFE ITSELF!

You can't argue with life – you can't fight it or control it. Things happen and you just have to deal with it. Sometimes that can feel pretty scary.

It can feel scary in the future – you might get elephant flu (or whatever the latest health scare happens to be), you might be in a car accident, your family might sell up and move to Moldova.

It can feel scary in the past. Maybe someone close to you was ill or died, just like that, no warning, no explanation – just life doing its own thing.

It can feel scary right now – in fact, sometimes it might feel safer to stay in bed and pull the blankets up over your head like an ostrich hiding its head in the sand. Well I hate to tell you this, but it isn't.

No-one can ever be one hundred per cent safe from bad things happening, and that means there are only two ways you can play it:

- Cower in a corner – not great for your self-esteem.

- Be up for everything – go hero!

THE RIVER AND THE ROCK

Which one is stronger – the river or the rock? Don't worry, this isn't a geography test – I'm about to make a philosophical point!

The rock seems stronger because it's hard and solid whereas water just flows away, right? But actually, over time, the river keeps on flowing and the rock gets eroded away.

Are you a river or a rock? Do the quiz and find out.

THE ROCK-OR-RIVER QUIZ

1 Your grandpa's bought you a really expensive birthday present. Do you think

A He shouldn't have spent so much money on me.
B Yay! It's just what I wanted!

2 You're supposed to be having a picnic but it's started to rain. Do you think

A I shouldn't have bothered making sandwiches.
B Let's have a picnic indoors instead.

3 Your teacher says your project is the best in the class. Do you think

A She should have chosen Paul's – it's much better.
B When you're good, you're good!

4 You've broken your right arm. Do you think

A Prince shouldn't have been lying on the stairs.
B I'd better learn to write with my left hand.

5 Your mum buys your favourite breakfast cereal with marshmallow pieces for a treat. Do you think

A She should buy it for me every day.
B Yum!

RESULTS

Mostly As: You're like a rock resisting life by wanting things to be how you think they should be, instead of how they are. You're going to get worn down!

Mostly Bs : You're flowing with the river of life – and that makes you unstoppable!

· ·

If you want to be strong, flow with the river of life – don't try to block it. Accept everything that happens, and let it carry you forward. When great things happen, be glad and grateful. These are life's gifts, so don't reject them by feeling that you have to deserve them. Good things are like a sunny day – they just happen, so get out there and enjoy them!

When bad things happen, they are life's gifts too, even though you'd probably like to give them back. Accept them, explore them and find out what they can do for you. In the immortal words of the Rolling Stones (your grandpa's probably got the record):

> **You can't always get what you want…**
> **but you get what you need**

LIFE'S LESSONS

When things happen that you don't want to happen, that puts you outside your comfort zone and you have to develop new skills to deal with it. These are life skills and life's lessons.

It's like learning stuff at school – you might think you'd rather keep doing decimals because you understand them and therefore you always get ten out of ten. But, although getting top marks makes you happy on the short term, it isn't enough.

Unless you want to do decimals every week until you leave school, sooner or later you have to move outside your comfort zone and let your teacher start a new topic, even though at first she might as well be talking in Portuguese.

When life feels uncomfortable it always means there's something for you to learn – even if it's simply that you can cope and find strategies for dealing with it.

Jasmine

When Jasmine found out that her best friend, Summer, was leaving, it felt like the end of the world. The two of them had always been so close that they'd never bothered to make any other friends, so who would she hang out with at school now? And how would she fill her evenings and weekends? It was a catastrophe!

But when Summer had gone, the other girls tried to cheer Jasmine up, and soon she was being invited to hang out with them after school. She still missed Summer, of course, but most days they had a long chat on their mobiles and there was loads of new stuff to talk about, which was great. Sometimes they sent each other little gifts and cards, and organised weekend visits to each other's houses.

Jasmine still wished that Summer hadn't had to leave, but when it happened she had found out that she could manage on her own and get new mates, and that friends can still be close even if there's 50 miles between them.

The more you cope with difficult things, the stronger you get, like building up muscle in the gym. If you never have to deal with disappointment, loss, frustration and all that bad stuff, you stay flabby and weak. You feel fearful too because, if you've never been tested, how can you feel confident that you will be OK?

So take everything life throws at you – don't try to duck and dive. If it's fun, enjoy it! If it hurts, look for the lesson. That's how you can harness the astonishing power of life itself and allow it to make you the most that you can be.

TEN WAYS TO SAY YES TO LIFE

Going with the flow of life is a way of boosting your self-esteem. Here are ten ways to start saying yes to life.

1. Real life – the past

Regret, guilt, anger and sadness are all ways of holding onto the past. You can't flow with the river if you're holding on to the sides. Here's a little ritual that will help you to let go.

1. Think of something in the past that you wish hadn't happened – everyone has plenty to choose from.

2. Write down what happened or do it as a picture strip.

3. When you've finished, scrunch it up and bury it in the garden, or tear it up into tiny pieces and throw it away.

2. Go with the flow

Do this lying down with your eyes shut, either on your bed or in a lovely warm bath. Start with three long, slow breaths to calm yourself.

Imagine you're floating downstream in a sparkling river, as light as a leaf, unsinkable. Sometimes you come to rapids and waterfalls, and maybe it gets a bit scary, and sometimes you come to quiet pools full of sunlight.

It's impossible to resist the flow of the river, so let go and enjoy the ride all the way down to the sea.

3. Real life – the future

The future is an idea. No one knows for sure what's going to happen, so worrying is a waste of time.

It's no more sensible to expect bad things than good things, so throughout the day, whenever you catch yourself worrying about bad things happening – 'What if I fail my test?', 'Supposing I catch Gemma's cold?', 'There might be a terrorist attack on my school' – STOP!

See how it feels to confidently expect everything to turn out fine.

4. Make lemonade!

'When life sends you lemons, make lemonade!' as the saying goes.

Make some lemonade and see how you can transform a bitter experience (have you ever tried sucking a lemon?) into something delicious.

LOVELY LEMONADE

Squeeze one lemon and put the juice in a tall glass. Add one level dessert spoon of sugar. Fill the glass with water nearly to the top and stir until the sugar's dissolved. Pop an ice cube in it and enjoy!

5. It's all great today!

Be positive about everything that happens throughout the day. Even if something upsets or annoys you think 'What can I learn?'

Warning: This can be a hard one. It's bad enough when your best mate's banging on about her new crush or your teacher's in a bad mood. These are little lessons in patience and tolerance. But big lessons take much longer, like if your auntie's really ill or your mum and dad are splitting up. With big problems the learning isn't instant – your job right now is to trust that it will make you stronger in the end.

6. Be not-fair-aware

One of the commonest ways of arguing with life is grumbling about things not being fair. Life isn't fair, end of.

List five things you envy in people you know – 'Finn's season ticket', 'Sasha's trainers', 'Miss

Dobson's cleverness', 'Jamie's house', 'Jo's hair'.

Now list five things other people might envy in you – 'My new mobile', 'my family life', 'the way I make people laugh', 'the fact that I live near the beach...', 'My hamster, Fang'

The things you envy in other people give you something to aim for and the things they might envy in you give you something to be grateful for.

7. The 'Mighty me!' pic

You'll need a piece of card – the back of a cereal packet will do. Plus some old newspapers, pens, scissors and a glue stick.

1. Fold the card in half, then open it again.

2. Draw yourself in the middle so your waist is about on the fold.

3. Cut or tear some disaster headlines out of newspapers and magazines and stick them on the card around the picture of yourself. If you prefer, make up your own headlines and write them around it, or do both – 'Flu pandemic hits Europe', 'School bus crash', 'Fang goes missing...'

4. Cut all around the picture of yourself above the fold line.

5. Fold over like a card on either side of the figure, and watch yourself rise above all those disasters!

8. Life's thank you letter

Write a thank-you letter to life for all the great gifts that you've received during the day. 'Dear Life, Thank-you for cornflakes and also Dad's joke (What's a sea monster's favourite meal? Fish and ships – ba boom!) Thank you for my mate Marigold…'

9. The 'I handled it' tick list

Write down 5 difficult things you've been through in your life. Have you ever been ill or been bullied, or lost a friend? Have you had to move house or change your family set-up? Have you really looked forward to something that never came about? Or wanted something you never got? Then ask yourself, are you still alive?

Put a tick beside each one of them to show you handled it.

10. The 'Ho hum' haiku

Haiku have three lines
five syllables, then seven
and five to finish

If something makes you feel fed up today… ho hum… Turn it into a haiku. Creating pictures, music and poems out of bad stuff is one way of making it into something good.

It was chips for tea
There wasn't any ketchup
I got in a mood

CHAPTER SEVEN
CELEBRATE BEING YOU!

Do you ever think stuff like, 'Why can't I look cool like my sister?' and 'Why can't I be brainy like my mate Ben?' and 'Why can't I be jolly all the time like the kid next door?'

Wanting to be the same as other people is a sort of self-rejection, and that's not good news for your self-esteem. It's also silly because life just isn't like that.

It reminds me of a joke:

> Why is an elephant big, grey and wrinkly?
>
> Because if it was small, white and smooth, it would be a ping-pong ball.

If elephants were the same as ping-pong balls, who'd want to go on safari? And if ping pong balls were the same as elephants...

If you were as cool as your sister or as brainy as your mate or as jolly as your neighbour, you wouldn't be you, and that would be a sad loss to all of us. It's our differences that make life interesting.

EVERYONE'S DIFFERENT – YIPPEE!

Here are five ways we're all different from each other and five reasons why that's great.

1. Appearance
People come in all shapes, sizes and colours, and different bodies have different strengths and weaknesses.

That's great because...
...if everyone looked the same we wouldn't be able to tell who was who! And if everyone's body

could do the same stuff, the Olympics would go on forever.

2. Emotional climate

Emotions are a bit like the weather. We all get sunny days and dull days, storms and depressions. But different people have different emotional climates, just like some places tend to be more dry and sunny, and others more warm and wet.

You might be naturally cool and calm, or moody and changeable, or bubbly and bright, and fighting that would be as sensible as trying to start a ski school in Cornwall.

But it's great because...

...if everyone was cool and calm there wouldn't be much excitement in the world and if everyone was moody and changeable no-one would get a minute's peace! Different sorts of people balance each other out.

3. Thinking style

If you're a logical thinker, you work things out. 'Mum gave me £5 so let me see – if I spend £3 on a sandwich, £1 on a drink and 50p on a cereal bar that means...'

If you're an intuitive thinker, you might not be so good at working it out but you don't need to because you're great at guessing. 'Sandwich, drink, cereal bar – that feels about right!'

It's great having different thinking styles because...
...if everyone thought logically, there'd be a world shortage of flashes of inspiration, and if everyone thought intuitively, nothing would ever get completed.

4. Tastes
We've all got different tastes in music, clothes, food and so on.

That's great because...
...it means we have masses of choice, because shops and industries have to meet lots of different demands.

5. Voice
I don't just mean the sound of your voice – though come to think of it, I do like the fact that Geordies speak one way and Welsh people another, and I do like that my gran (soft, gentle) didn't sound the same as my grandpa (gravely, deep). By 'voice', I mean how you express yourself in the world. Some people sing or write poems or draw pictures. Some people express themselves more physically, through sport or body language.

Everyone expressing themselves in different ways is great because...

…if you're more of a musician, say, or a touchy-feely person, you need writing types like me to give you something to read, and if I want some nice tunes when I'm driving around or a hug when I'm feeling fed up, I need musical and physical types like you.

There are masses of ways we're all different and masses of reasons to be glad about it, but people can still try to make you conform and be like everybody else. Peer pressure is particularly bad at school.

Elliott

Elliott's favourite way of spending break times was sitting at the edge of the school field with his notebook, writing poems. As you can imagine, the other boys didn't think much of that, and they didn't think much of Elliott. They were always teasing him.

Elliott's teacher was worried about him and she wouldn't believe that he was perfectly happy on his own. She kept trying to make him tell her what was wrong.

Eventually Elliott started thinking that maybe there was something wrong with him and then he tried to join in more, but his heart wasn't in it and therefore he wasn't very good at it and he felt more like a miserable misfit than ever.

One day, when he just couldn't stand it any more, he went out with his notebook at break-time and wrote a poem called 'Being me.' He wanted people to understand what he felt when he was out there on his own, and the words came cascading through his mind like a sunlit stream full of rainbows.

When Elliott's poem won first prize in a national competition, people stopped trying to make him change. If they saw him scribbling away at the far corner of the field they would just say, 'I wonder what Elliott is writing about today.'

Some people feel threatened by difference because they don't like things they don't understand. But if we were all the same, we'd die of boredom!

Therefore, enjoy your uniqueness. Don't wish that you could be somebody else.

TEN WAYS TO CELEBRATE BEING YOU

It's easy to feel different from other people, but it can be hard to feel glad about that. Feeling happy to be yourself is one way to boost your self-esteem – and here are ten ways to celebrate being you.

1. Happy birthday!
Your birthday is part of your identity. Draw

yourself as a baby and put the day, month and year of your birth underneath.

What time of year is it? If you were born in the spring or summer, put yourself in a garden with flowers and trees. If you were born in the autumn or winter, give yourself a nice warm blanket by the fireside.

This is how the world looked when you first opened your eyes. Summer babies come into a world of open air, sunshine, outdoors sounds and smells, but the world for winter babies is an indoors place, close and cosy.

No wonder we're all different when even members of the same family can be born into a different world!

2. Fifteen favourite foods

List your five favourite savoury foods, five favourite sweet foods and five favourite snacks. Yum!

Try to eat one from each section during the day.

Good idea: You might have a better chance of persuading your mum to make macaroni cheese and lemon pancakes for tea if you tell her, 'It says in my book they'll be good for my self-esteem.'

3. Five favourite people

List your five favourite people. Contact all of them in one day by:

- Seeing them
- Emailing
- Phoning
- Texting
- Sending a letter or card

4. Your favourite colour

What's your favourite colour? Mine's red. How dreary life would be without it!

Have a party, or sleepover, or family tea, to celebrate your favourite colour. Supposing it's green, send out green invitations telling everyone to come completely dressed in green and bring something green to eat.

5. Make your own music mix

Make a playlist of your favourite music, bands you like, Classical stuff, songs you used to sing along to in the car when you were little, whatever. Let it be a wonderful, magical mixture.

6. A pleasure shared...

...is a pleasure doubled!

Get one or two of your mates round for a 'favourite music' night. Ask everyone to bring a playlist of their three best tracks to talk about and listen to together.

Note: Sharing's great for other things as well. Why not have a 'favourite books' night with everyone bringing their best book to talk about, or 'favourite pictures' or 'favourite sitcom videos'?

7. Delight your senses

Taste, sight, hearing, smell and touch – those are the five senses. Jot down several things for each that you find pleasurable. For example –

Smell: hot chocolate, freshly cut grass, Big Ted, the sports hall

Touch: my woolly slipper socks, warm bath water, Big Ted, Dad's bristly chin

'One man's meat is another man's poison,' as they say, and everyone likes different things. It's part of your uniqueness if you like the smell of the sports hall and the feel of your dad's bristly chin.

8. The yuk factor

The things you don't like are part of your uniqueness too. Write another list of your five senses but this time put down all the things you hate. For example –

Hearing: the dog next door barking, Dad's Beethoven CD, Mum yelling at me, low-flying planes

Sight: Miss Harris's bright pink lipstick, the dog's bottom, that sick-coloured carpet in the quiet room at school...

9. All your names

You've probably got a lot more names than you think! Fill in this list and see.

- First name, including all its forms that people use for you (James, Jamie, Jimmy, Jim, Jay, J).

- Middle name.

- Surname.

- Mum's pet names for you (possibly 'darling' or 'sweetie' but often also quite random like 'Bobsie' and 'Floss').

- Dad's pet names for you (usually as weird as Mum's).

- Mates' nicknames for you.

- Brothers' and sisters' nicknames for you.

- The name you wish your parents had chosen for you.

- The one you're eternally grateful they didn't choose for you.

- The ones that got away (that is, what they

nearly called you but decided against it – you might have to ask them about those).

- Other names that don't fit into any of the above.

10. Just imagine...

'The real world' is something everybody shares but the world of the imagination is completely unique to you.

Just imagine for example that you could create a brand new breed of dog. Really picture it in your mind. Mine's got a green tail and hindquarters, and the front half of its body is yellow with green stripes. It's got long eyelashes and the hair on the top of its head is held back with a silver bow.

Draw a picture of your imaginary dog, or describe it in words. No one in the world has ever seen that dog except you. How amazing is that?

AND FINALLY...

Rome wasn't built in a day. If you want to build up your self-esteem you have to practice, and the reason why there are gazillions of tasks for you to try is that by the time you've done them all, feeling good about yourself will have started to become your normal habit. High five!

If you've enjoyed doing the tasks, there's no need to stop. You can do them again right away, or whenever you feel your self-esteem could do with a top-up. There are absolutely no unwanted side effects!

If you find any particular ones that work really well for you, make them part of your normal life. Lots of people throughout the world use things like mind messages, good deeds and little celebrations every day, to make themselves feel good. So can you.

Other books by Jenny Alexander

BULLIES, BIGMOUTHS AND SO-CALLED FRIENDS

This book doesn't just show you how to pretend you don't care – it shows you how to really not care – so you can get on with your own life and not let someone else's lack of social skills (that's putting it nicely!) spoil everything. Plus it's got lots of quizzes and cartoons and stuff, so it's a great read.

'Brilliant tips for children who may be struggling at school when the usual advice of 'ignore it' isn't working.' ***The Sun***

'Unique in teaching children how to boost their self-esteem and so prevent bullying from affecting their lives.' ***The Independent***

'No other author has done the job on the subject of bullying as well as Alexander does.' ***Junior Magazine***

GOING UP! THE NO-WORRIES GUIDE TO SECONDARY SCHOOL

Worries are a normal part of every new adventure – they're nature's way of making you prepare. One way of preparing is by getting information – and all the information you need about going up to secondary school is right here!

'The author knows what makes Y6 laugh – the jokes are really good!'
Ben Amberley-Smith, 11, quoted in *The Teacher*

'Tackles common problems and worries in a positive and reassuring manner that will help to prepare pupils for their now school environment.'
Headteacher Update

'I think this book is really great (and funny!). I myself am going to secondary school this September and I read this and it helped me.'
I review books!

HOW TO BE A BRILLIANT WRITER

Not as in, how to get great SAT results, but as in how to make writing a brilliant part of your everyday life (though actually doing lots of writing for fun means your SAT results will get better all on their own)

'An essential guide for young, aspiring writers.'
Headteacher Update

'A book that should capture children's imagination, make them realise that writing can be fun, and inspire them to create their own written material.'
Writing Magazine

HOW 2B HAPPY

Everyone gets down in the dumps sometimes – it's only natural – but this book shows you how to bounce back quicker and develop a happy lifestyle. Plus it's got lots of quizzes, cartoons, stories and jokes ☺

HOW TO GET WHAT YOU WANT, BY PEONY PINKER.

If you like funny stories about families, pets and friends, you'll love reading the Peony Pinker books – and you'll pick up lots of useful tips along the way!

As well as 'How to get what you want, by Peony Pinker', you can read 'How to get the friends you want', 'How to get the family you want' and 'How to get the body you want', all by Peony Pinker, too.

'Entertaining and humorous… if you have readers looking for an alternative to Jacqueline Wilson, then introduce them to Peony.'
The School Librarian

'In the second hilarious instalment in the life of one Peony Pinker, the plucky heroine is seriously fed up with her family. But how can she go about changing their annoying traits? Find out in this funny, family read.' ***tBkmag***

'The Peony Pinker stories combine humour and an unexpected narrative with subtle tips on how to get the best from life.' ***Western Morning News***

ALSO IN THE 70 WAYS SERIES

70 WAYS to BULLY-PROOF YOURSELF

Banish those bullies!

JENNY ALEXANDER

Printed in Great Britain
by Amazon